In Front Of or Behind

Where's Eddie?

Daniel Nunn

Illustrations by Steve Walker

Raintree

HAMMERSMITH AND FULHAM

Hide and Seek

www.raintreepublishers.co.uk
Visit our website to find out
more information about
Raintree books.

To order:
☎ Phone 0845 6044371
🖹 Fax +44 (0) 1865 312263
🖴 Email myorders@raintreepublishers.co.uk

Customers from outside the UK please telephone +44 1865 312262

Raintree is an imprint of Capstone Global Library Limited,
a company incorporated in England and Wales having its
registered office at 7 Pilgrim Street, London, EC4V 6LB –
Registered company number: 6695582

Text © Capstone Global Library Limited 2013
First published in hardback in 2013
First published in paperback in 2014
The moral rights of the proprietor have been asserted.

Edited by Dan Nunn, Rebecca Rissman, and Sian Smith
Designed by Joanna Hinton-Malivoire
Picture research by Mica Brancic
Originated by Capstone Global Library Ltd.
Production by Victoria Fitzgerald
Printed and bound in China by Leo Paper Products Ltd

ISBN 978 1 406 23895 2 (hardback)
16 15 14 13 12
10 9 8 7 6 5 4 3 2 1

ISBN 978 1 406 23901 0 (paperback)
17 16 15 14 13
10 9 8 7 6 5 4 3 2 1

British Library Cataloguing in Publication Data
Nunn, Daniel.
  In front of or behind : where's Eddie?. – (Hide and seek)
  1. English language–Synonyms and antonyms–Pictorial
  works–Juvenile literature.
  I. Title II. Series
  428.1-dc23

Acknowledgements
We would like to thank the following for permission to reproduce
photographs: Shutterstock pp.5 (© Losevsky Pavel), 6 (© Dmitry
Rukhlenko), 7 (© jomphong), 8 (© nito), 9 (© Tungphoto), 10 (©
Ihnatovich Maryia), 11, 12 (© vseb), 13, 14 (© WDG Photo), 15, 16
(© craftvision), 17, 18 (© Tomaz Kunst), 19, 20 (© Valentina R.), 21
(© Tihis), 22 (© Valentina R.), 23 (© Dudarev Mikhail).

Front cover photograph of cupcakes reproduced with permission
of Shutterstock (© Elena Talberg). Back cover photograph of a
sandcastle reproduced with permission of Shutterstock (© nito).

Every effort has been made to contact copyright holders of any
material reproduced in this book. Any omissions will be rectified in
subsequent printings if notice is given to the publisher.

2

Contents

Meet Eddie the Elephant 4

In front of 6

Behind 8

Find Eddie! 10

True or false? 21

Answers and more! 24

Be careful when you hide!
Eddie can hide in places where people can't. Hiding inside things can be very dangerous. Always ask an adult if it is safe first.

Meet Eddie the Elephant

This is Eddie the Elephant.

Eddie loves to play hide and seek!

In front of

Sometimes Eddie hides in front of things.

6

Behind

Sometimes Eddie hides **behind** things.

When you are **behind** something,
that thing is **in front of** you.

Find Eddie!

Can you find Eddie?
Count to 10, then off you go!

Where is Eddie? Is he **in front of** the hippo or **behind** the hippo?

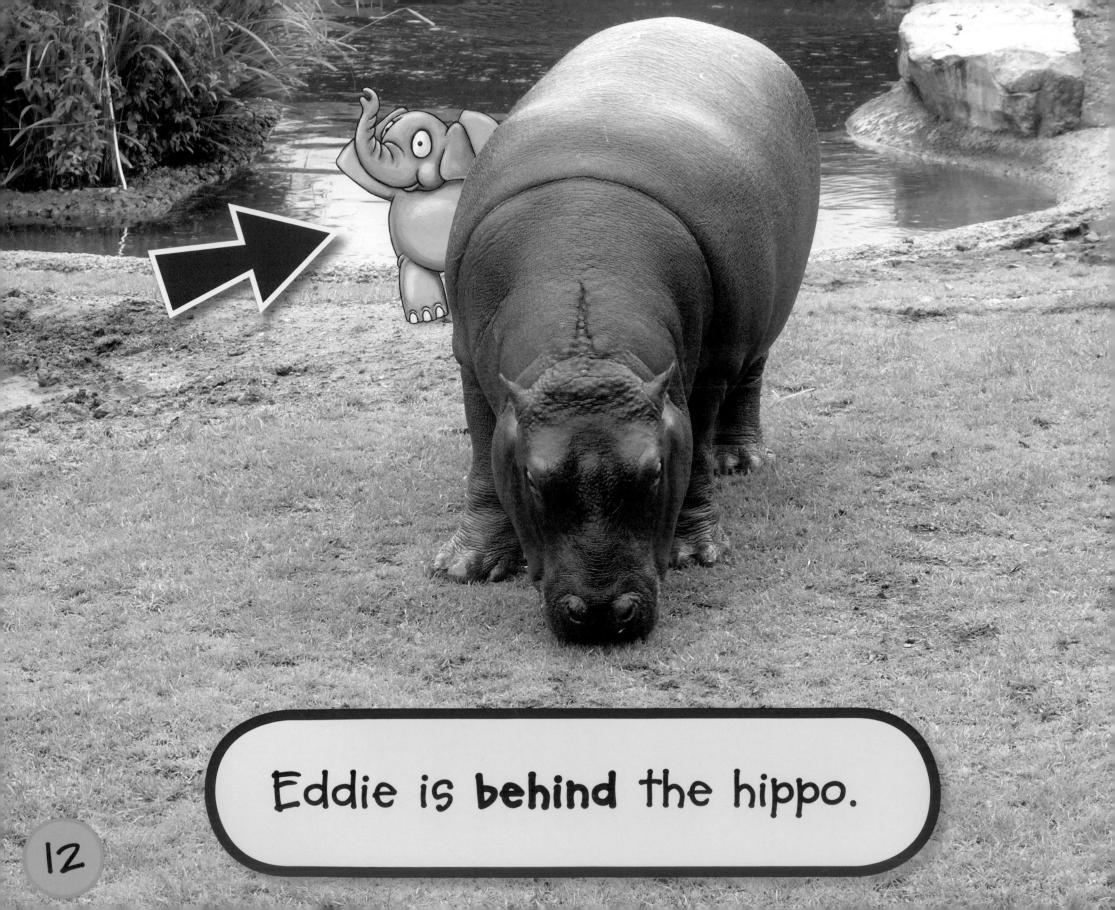

Eddie is **behind** the hippo.

Where is Eddie? Is he **in front of** the tree or **behind** the tree?

13

Where is Eddie?

Is he **in front of** the bouncy castle or **behind** the bouncy castle?

Eddie is **in front of** the bouncy castle.

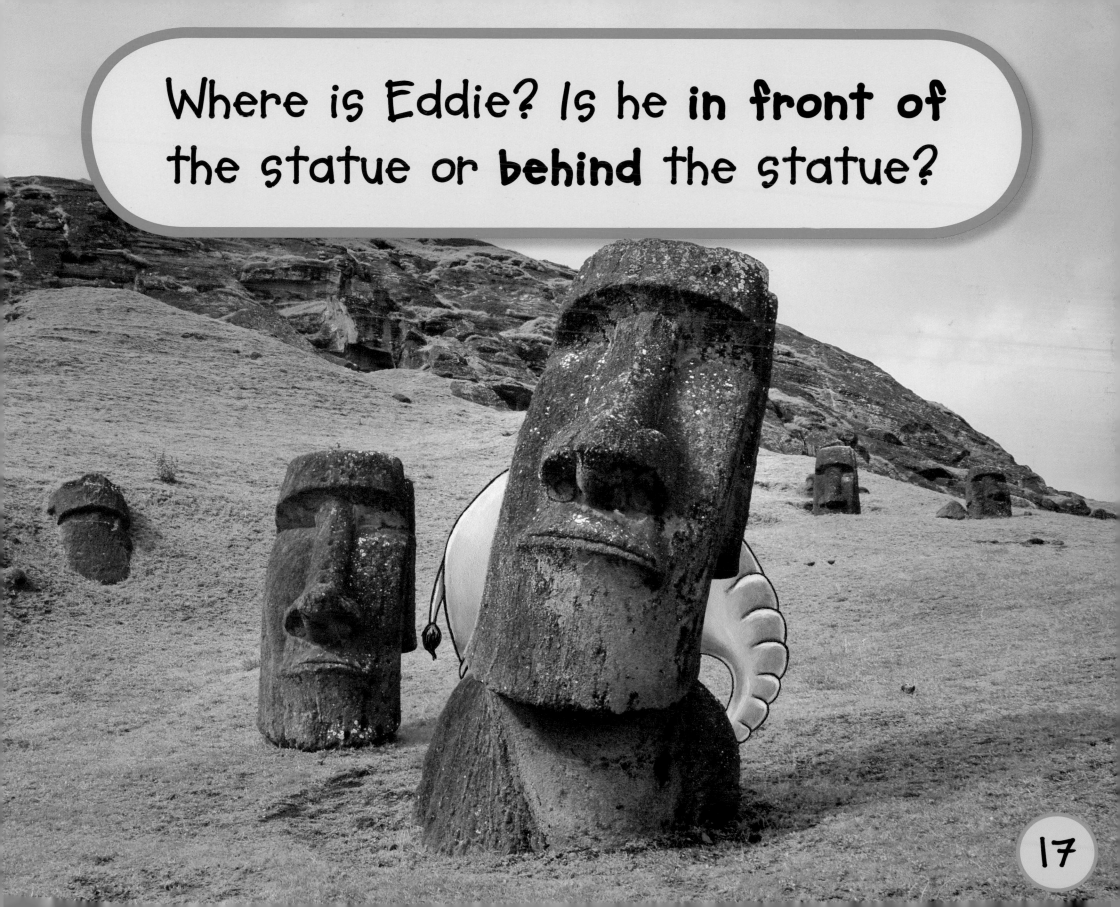

Where is Eddie? Is he **in front of** the statue or **behind** the statue?

Where is Eddie? Is he **in front of** the apple or **behind** the apple?

Eddie is **behind** the apple.

True or false?

1. Eddie is **in front of** the snowman. True or false?

You can find the answers on page 24.

2. Eddie is **in front of** the teddy.
True or false?

22

3. Eddie is **behind**
   the bicycle.
   True or false?

True or false?

1. True! Eddie is **in front of** the snowman.
2. False! Eddie is **behind** the teddy.
3. False! Eddie is **in front of** the bicycle.

Where can Eddie hide next?

Look around the room you are in.

What could Eddie hide **in front of**?

What could Eddie hide **behind**?